Building Literacy Skills
Vowel Sounds

Editor
Eric Migliaccio

Managing Editor
Ina Massler Levin, M.A.

Editor-in-Chief
Sharon Coan, M.S. Ed.

Cover Artist
Barb Lorseyedi

Art Manager
Kevin Barnes

Art Director
CJae Froshay

Imaging
Ralph Olmedo, Jr.
Temo Parra
Rosa C. See

Product Manager
Phil Garcia

Publishers
Rachelle Cracchiolo, M.S. Ed.
Mary Dupuy Smith, M.S. Ed.

Author

Gilly Czerwonka

Teacher Created Materials, Inc.
6421 Industry Way
Westminster, CA 92683
www.teachercreated.com.
ISBN-0-7439-3240-4

©2004 Teacher Created Materials, Inc.
Made in U.S.A.

The classroom teacher may reproduce copies of materials in this book for classroom use only. The reproduction of any part for an entire school or school system is strictly prohibited. No part of this publication may be transmitted, stored, or recorded in any form without written permission from the publisher.

This edition is published with © Folens Limited

First published 2001 by Folens Limited.

United Kingdom: Folens Publishers, Apex Business Center, Boscombe Road, Dunstable, LU5 4RL.

Email: folens@folens.com

Gilly Czerwonka hereby asserts her moral right to be identified as the author of this work in accordance with the Copyright, Designs and Patents Act 1988.

Editor: Nicky Platt

Layout artist: Patricia Hollingsworth

Cover design: Martin Cross

© 2001 Folens Limited, on behalf of the authors.

Every effort has been made to contact copyright holders of material used in this publication. If any copyright holder has been overlooked, we should be pleased to make any necessary arrangements.

Table of Contents—Book 3

Using the *Building Basic Literacy Skills* Series 6

General Guidelines for Good Practice 11

Unit 1: Two Vowels Together 12
Dividing Syllables—Matching Syllables—Using Two Vowels Together—Compound Words—Two Vowel Poetry—Unit 1 Word List

Unit 2: Vowels and Word Endings 18
Using "y" as a Vowel—The Suffixes "ly" and "ty"—Adding "es" and "ing"—Making "y" Words Plural—Words with "ight"—"y" Word Poetry—Unit 2 Word List

Unit 3: "ew" and "oo" 25
Reading "ew" and "oo"—Writing with "ew" and "oo"—Two-Syllable "oo" Words—More "oo," "ew," and "ui"—"ew," and "oo" Poetry—Unit 3 Word List

Unit 4: "ou"/"ow" and "oi"/"oy" 31
Words with "ou" and "ow"—More Words with "ou" and "ow"—Words with "oi" and "oy"—More Words with "oi" and "oy"—Vowel-Sound Poetry—Unit 4 Word List

Unit 5: Three-Syllable Vowel Sounds 37
Three-Syllable Words—Dividing Three Syllables—Using Three-Syllable Words—Understanding Three-Syllable Words—Three-Syllable Poetry—Unit 5 Word List

Student Target Sheets 43
Student Target Sheets—Tutor's Instructions for Student Target Sheet—Student Target Sheet—Certificate of Achievement

Appendices 47
Appendix 1: Graph of Reading Speed—*Appendix 2:* The "Self Voice" Method—*Appendix 3:* Phonic Spell Checks—*Appendix 4:* Phonic Checklist—*Appendix 5:* Phonic Spell Check for Consonant Blends—*Appendix 6:* Sound Cards—*Appendix 7:* Cards for Word Games

Answer Key 73

Introduction to the Series

Building Basic Literacy Skills is a complete course for students in the early years of middle school. It has been divided into seven books for ease of use by teachers, tutors, and students. **This is *Book 3: Vowel Sounds*.** The following is a summary of the contents of each of the seven books in the series.

Book 1: Words
- covers the building and splitting of simple c-v-c (consonant-vowel-consonant) combinations and consonant blends

Book 2: Syllables
- covers breaking words into syllables and long vowel sounds

Book 3: Vowel Sounds
- covers the long vowel combinations and splitting syllables with long vowel sounds

Book 4: Word Beginnings and Endings
- deals with common prefixes and suffixes

Book 5: Complex Words
- deals with more complex multi-syllabic words and further common prefixes and suffixes

Book 6: Irregular Words
- deals with words that follow less common, or seemingly no, spelling patterns (often called "high frequency" vocabulary)

Book 7: Spelling
- comprises material for the checking and recording of progress in the spelling of words learned, through simple tests and activities

The units in the books work well when taught in order. If determined appropriate by the teacher, however, the units are designed so that they can be used in any order.

- Many students enter the middle-school phase of school unable to take full control of their reading—and more particularly their spelling—from a lack of knowledge of how letters work within words. If this is uncorrected, the sheer volume of reading and writing demanded during the middle-school years may leave them at a severe disadvantage.

- For some of these students, their potential for understanding information is marred by an inability to work quickly and automatically to decode and encode words. The *Building Basic Literacy Skills* program is designed to help them.

Introduction to the Series *(cont.)*

- Set out in unit lessons, it is aimed as a "second chance" for students who require extra support in basic understanding of the phonics, word, and syllable knowledge needed for reading and spelling.

- The units are designed to be delivered through extra daily sessions which may be monitored by a teacher, support teacher, support assistant, or tutor.

- Each unit follows a similar pattern of delivery, enabling students to work with the minimum of tutor preparation and guidance.

- Optimum group size will be dependent on the rate and speed at which the students gain understanding, but the program has been tested with full classes working in sub-groups under the overall guidance of one staff member.

Reading and writing performance have been closely linked to the phonemic knowledge of the student. The use of phonemic recording is critical because it acts as a self-teaching mechanism. It enables the learner to independently identify new words and thereby acquire the orthographic representations necessary for rapid autonomous visual word recognition. Simple exposure to the alphabetic orthography is not sufficient for a child to induce alphabetic principles spontaneously.

There are basically three types of readers. There are those who read phonetically, those who read whole words, and those who use a combination of the two methods. A combination of phonics and "whole word" reading is what a good reader uses.

Poor readers may try to read phonetically but do not have the knowledge of sound–symbol correspondence to allow them to be successful. Sound-symbol correspondence must be learned before any progress will be made.

"Whole word" readers do not recognize the individual letters or groups of letters that make up a word. They look at the outside shape of the word and match this from the shapes of whole words in their memory. Their competence with reading and spelling may then be dependent on the capacity of their memory. They may know some phonics but never use them to help with reading. "Whole word" readers are thought to make up 60% of all poor readers. To improve their reading and spelling they must learn sound–symbol correspondence. Using known words and getting them to identify sounds within the words is the way to start.

The *Building Basic Literacy Skills* program can be used with all types of readers. It teaches the reading, spelling, and contextual use of single- and multi-syllable words through a systematic progression of skills. Each unit focuses on a distinct group of skills: phonic, "whole word," or syllable division methods. Teaching strategies are common throughout the program.

Building Basic Literacy Skills is a structured and sequential program that begins with the identification of vowel and consonant letters of the alphabet and quickly extends to include strategies for attempting to read and spell unknown words. It is cumulative, as each new unit draws on skills and abilities already developed and so allows for new knowledge to be incorporated into the old.

Building Basic Literacy Skills was originally written to teach strategies for reading and spelling to underachieving students of middle-school age. It is, however, suitable for all ages from nine to ninety.

Using the *Building Basic Literacy Skills* Series

These general notes should be read before following the "Procedures for Working" on page 8.

✣ Level of Knowledge Assumed

To use the *Building Basic Literacy Skills*, students need to know and be able to recite the letters of the alphabet. They need to know the basic sounds of each consonant as it occurs at the beginning of a word. They need to know the "short" sounds of each vowel. (It is helpful but not necessary for them to know the terms "vowel" and "consonant.")

✣ Organizing and Working the Program

The program is designed so that it may be delivered with a complete class of lower-ability students. More often it has been used with groups of students who have been withdrawn from mainstream classrooms. It could also, of course, be used in a one-to-one or small group tutorial situation.

While it is perfectly possible that the later reinforcement and practice exercises in each unit may be completed as homework, it is important that a tutor be on hand to provide immediate support and feedback as students work.

Many tutors have also found it beneficial for students to work with a partner, who may be at the same stage or, in some cases, in advance of their partner on the program. Discussion with other students about the tasks in question and about progress is particularly important.

The program should be overseen by certified classroom teachers, but day-to-day operation could be monitored by a support assistant. This person is referred to throughout as "the tutor."

✣ Teaching the Program

Each unit begins with guided tutor-led material. The tutor leads the discussion, always beginning from a known point and linking this with the students' previous experience and knowledge. The starting point may be reviewing the work from the previous lesson.

The tutor models any new procedure on the board, talking through the examples shown. He or she then works through the procedure together with the students. Worksheets can be photocopied onto acetate and used on an overhead projector directed onto a whiteboard. Students can then be asked to complete the worksheets on the board first before they are given independent practice. Students may work in small groups for this phase. Working with others reduces anxiety suffered by individuals as the group solves any problem. The combined knowledge of the group will give an increase in the range of expertise available to an individual student.

Once tutors are sure that the children can read and understand the instructions and tasks that follow, the students may proceed at their own pace.

The last ten minutes of each lesson are given to review and class discussion of the work completed.

Using the *Building Basic Literacy Skills* Series (cont.)

✣ Reading Instructions

- Instructions boxed and marked with an "**i**" are intended, in the initial stages of the program, to be read by the tutor. They will often require demonstration to ensure that the students understand the new information. As the students progress through the program—and begin to work at their own pace—it is important that they fully understand these boxed instructions, since they introduce each new step. It is important that a tutor be on hand to check understanding and provide guidance.

- Where a "**r**" icon is included, the material in the box needs to be learned and retained by the students. The tutor might want to instruct that the students copy it into a "Spelling Rules" notebook.

- All other instructions are intended to be read, aloud if necessary, by the students themselves. Through the initial units of the program it may be helpful if the tutor checks that the students can read, understand, and follow the instructions carefully. There may also be occasions when the tutor will wish to read out loud the examples before the children complete the tasks. Later, students should work together, where possible, to read instructions and check understanding of sample sentences.

- Since the program is cumulative, practice in reading these instructions for themselves will help students to build up a vocabulary of basic sight words, including many of those necessary to follow instructions in other subjects. Reading these instructions for themselves also helps the students build confidence and independence and highlights the overall importance of reading and following instructions in their work.

- Single letters, vowels, or consonant blends surrounded by brackets indicate that they say their phonetic sound.

✣ Answer Key

The program is largely self-checking and typical answers for each unit are to be found on the answer pages located at the back of each book.

Since the students are actively encouraged to take control of their own learning, it may be sensible for the tutor to allow them to mark and grade their own work. This may be done by encouraging students to exchange papers to mark a partner's work. This will again involve reading and following instructions, and in itself may encourage the students to think more carefully about the patterns of letters within words.

Icon Review

i This icon indicates **instructions** to be read by the tutor.

r This icon indicates materials that need to be learned and **retained** by the students.

Using the *Building Basic Literacy Skills* Series *(cont.)*

Procedures for Working

Each unit should be worked through in sequential order to ensure all reading and spelling strategies are taught. The working procedures for all units are very similar and follow this progression:

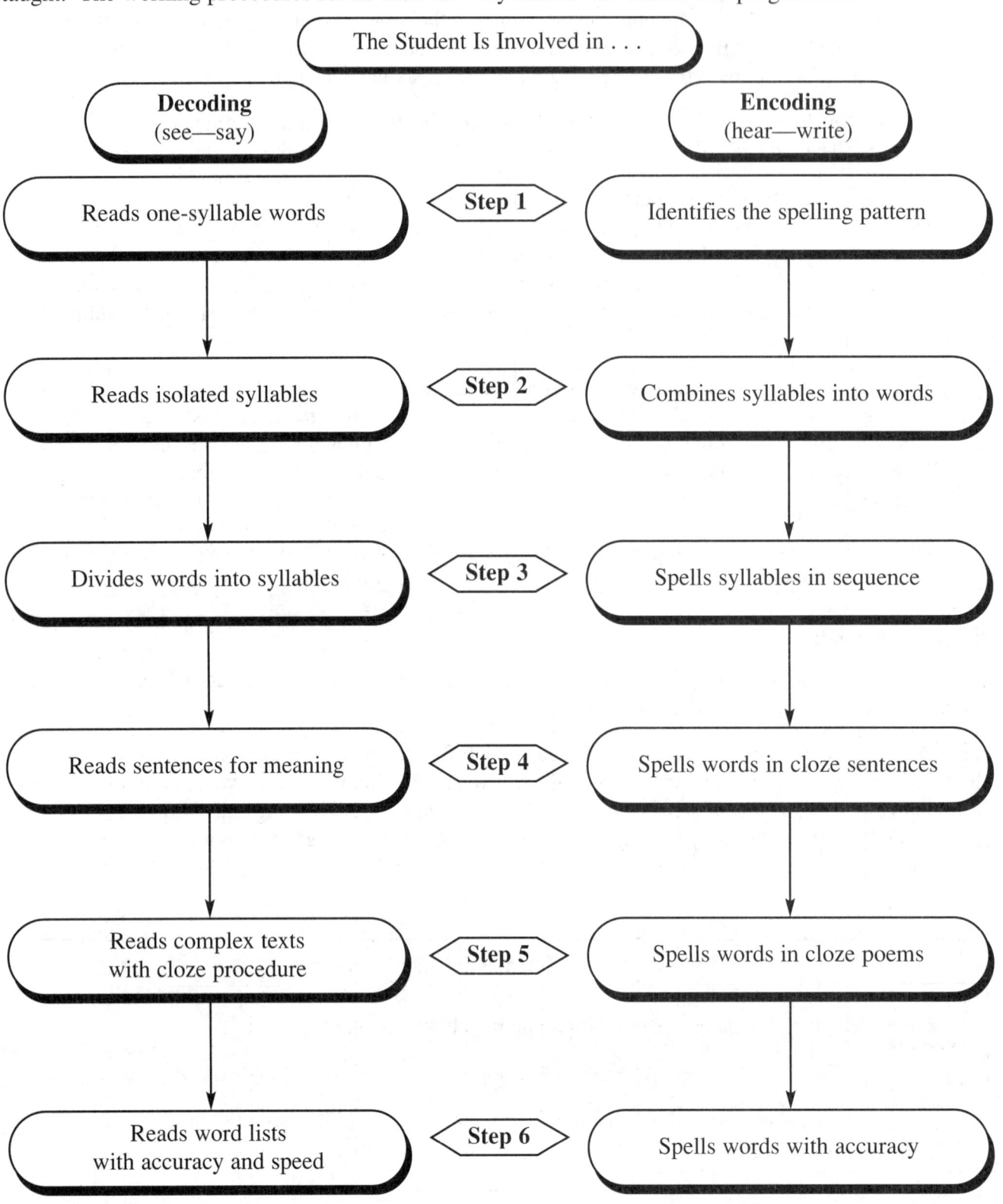

The Student Is Involved in . . .

Decoding (see—say) | | **Encoding** (hear—write)

Decoding		Encoding
Reads one-syllable words	Step 1	Identifies the spelling pattern
Reads isolated syllables	Step 2	Combines syllables into words
Divides words into syllables	Step 3	Spells syllables in sequence
Reads sentences for meaning	Step 4	Spells words in cloze sentences
Reads complex texts with cloze procedure	Step 5	Spells words in cloze poems
Reads word lists with accuracy and speed	Step 6	Spells words with accuracy

Using the *Building Basic Literacy Skills* Series (cont.)

❖ Word Lists

For reading, the goal is to teach word-attack skills so students can use them when decoding unfamiliar words. New, unfamiliar words are then included that will challenge their understanding of the strategies taught. The vocabulary is not limited. Each unit ends with Word Lists that follow the pattern of that unit. These words can be made into word cards to use for playing word games in school or at home.

The student is asked to read the Word List daily along with, or to, a peer, parent/guardian, or helper. The number of words read within one minute should be plotted on a graph for that unit (provided in Appendix 1 on page 48). The graph gives a very clear indicator to the student and tutor of the improvement in the automaticity of visual word recognition.

Spelling is a more complex skill and difficult to master. The number of spellings given to learn from the word list will depend on the literacy level of the student. The words chosen should be those the students most commonly use.

Students should be questioned intermittently to check that they understand the vocabulary used in the program. The students maintain a record of their work by keeping a checklist on the Student Target Sheet. Each unit can be supplemented by using selected words from the word lists to write sentences, find their meanings in a dictionary, and find rhyming words.

❖ Poems

The poems included towards the end of each unit have been deliberately printed in complex type. (Some non-dyslexic adults may find this makes it more difficult for them to read!) This graphic structure prevents "whole word" reading of the words and therefore activates the perceptual (right) side of the brain. Each letter has to be identified visually and so phonics comes into play.

The poems also utilize the **cloze** procedure. *Cloze*—which is sometimes called the sentence completion technique—works by deleting a word from a line of poetry and asking the students to supply the missing part. The purpose of the cloze procedure is to ensure the student uses semantic and syntactic cues by choosing the correct word to "fit" each line of the poem. This process involves the linguistic (left) side of the brain. Pupils have to make sense of what they have read to be able to complete the poems successfully.

If pupils find reading the poems very difficult they are asked to read the single words only. The tutor or a partner may read the poem and ask the student to "fit" the correct word into each line. The poems at the end of each unit of work can be completed as a class activity, providing opportunities for discussion.

Children and adults who read and spell with confidence have the ability to "play" with language. They can understand and take pleasure from a pun, spoonerism, or other play on words. *Building Basic Literacy Skills* endeavors to encourage this ability by including sentences and poems that are deliberately off-beat. Since many of the students will have failed already in "traditional" phonics-based approaches and may see these earlier programs as infantile, these jokes with language should be encouraged and shared. It is quite possible that in order to gain respect for the English language we also need to learn how to be disrespectful of it!

Using the *Building Basic Literacy Skills* Series (cont.)

❖ Timed Tasks

These tasks are marked with 🕐 .

The final task in each unit is intended as an assessment of what has been learned. If possible, the students should complete these tasks under pressure of time. Their aim should be to better their previous time rather than compete with other students' times. Tutors may prefer to give less able students a longer or unlimited time to complete the tasks.

❖ Student Target Sheets

It is important that the students complete the Student Target Sheet in cooperation with the tutor as they complete each unit.

There are four different areas to be assessed:

- completion of each worksheet
- answering of questions about the topics covered
- reading speed
- spelling.

The students can color in the units completed and the rules they have remembered correctly. The results of their reading and spelling checks are recorded in the right-hand columns.

The Student Target Sheet covers the five units of the program included in the book. A certificate can be given on its successful completion.

For students of very low ability it may be sensible to mask parts of the Student Target Sheet so that they complete one unit at a time. This should keep a small number of targets within their potential grasp.

❖ Appendices

Each book in the program contains appendices of informal assessment material to keep track of children's progress over the whole program. Appendices 1–6 may be used at any time to check a student's ability to progress through the units. Appendix 7 contains material related to each of the units.

General Guidelines for Good Practice

⇒ Familiarize yourself with the format of the program by working through the worksheets.

⇒ Take the literacy level of the students into account. Always ensure students are successful, either by limiting the amount of work to be completed, or by working through the units together.

⇒ Encourage the students to scan the whole page quickly before beginning each worksheet.

⇒ Make sure that students work in a logical manner, left to right, across the page.

⇒ Ensure that students read and follow the instructions properly.

⇒ Always encourage cursive script.

⇒ When choosing words from a list to complete a cloze passage, insist the students mark off the words as they use them.

⇒ Always encourage the re-reading of work to make sure the sentences and passages make sense.

⇒ Ensure consolidation of the phonemic pattern of letters or letter strings previously taught by frequently asking "what sound" the letters make.

⇒ The vocabulary in this program is not limited and will therefore contain some words not generally used by the students. Encourage the students to use a dictionary or spellchecker or ask for an explanation. You can use this opportunity to discuss these words with the group. (Be aware that using a dictionary may be very stressful for students with specific literacy or learning difficulties.)

⇒ Some students will always have difficulty voicing consonant blends. Do not let this hold up their progress, but place emphasis on the visual recognition of onsets.

Unit 1: Two Vowels Together

Dividing Syllables

To divide a word into syllables (beats):

- Find the vowels and mark them with the letter **v**.
- Mark the consonants between the vowels with the letter **c**.
- Split the word into two: **vc/cv**, **v/cv**, or **vc/v**.

1. Say the sound of the vowels and combine the syllables to make a word. Then look, say, listen, cover, write, and check!

a.

a	sleep	_____
cray	on	_____
de	cay	_____
re	veal	_____
con	tain	_____

b.

com	plaint	_____
re	peat	_____
be	tween	_____
un	load	_____
tea	cher	_____

2. Keeping the two vowels together, divide the words into syllables. Then look, say, listen, cover, write, and check!

	1st beat	2nd beat	Write the Word
obtain	_____	_____	_____
treatment	_____	_____	_____
coffee	_____	_____	_____
freedom	_____	_____	_____
beneath	_____	_____	_____
disease	_____	_____	_____
tweezers	_____	_____	_____
remain	_____	_____	_____

Unit 1: Two Vowels Together

Matching Syllables

1. Match the syllables to make a real word.

Mon	cay	_____
can	ish	_____
de	day	_____
tea	teen	_____
dis	leen	_____
six	cher	_____
squeam	teen	_____
Kath	ease	_____

2. Use the words above in the blanks. Then complete the story in your own words.

   Last _____ we found some maggots in the school's water _____. Someone had left meat to _____ on a plate near the canteen. The _____ said if we had eaten the meat we would have gotten a _____. There were _____ maggots wriggling about. I felt a bit _____, but _____ was sick on the spot! While the teacher was comforting her, Kevin picked up a maggot and put it _____

   _____ .

© Teacher Created Materials, Inc.   13   #3240 BBLS—Book 3: Vowel Sounds

Unit 1: Two Vowels Together

Using Two Vowels Together

1. Cross out the incorrect words in the sentences.

    a. There are seven **day days** in a week.

    b. Tony **cheat cheats cheated** in last year's exams.

    c. "Your school report was very **please pleased pleasing**, Tim."

    d. My teeth are **decay decays decaying** because I eat too many sweets.

    e. When I go on vacation this summer, I am **stay stays staying** in a hotel.

    f. Why do I always have to **repeat repeats repeating** myself?

    g. The shop was **display displays displaying** a selection of toys.

    h. He **appeal appealed appealing** to his mom to let him watch the television program.

2. Complete these sentences using your own words.

    a. I am very pleased about _____
    because I _____.

    b. The reason I am mad is because _____
    and you _____.

    c. When you have measles you have _____ and
    sometimes you _____.

    d. My dream is to _____
    so I _____.

#3240 BBLS—Book 3: Vowel Sounds   14   © Teacher Created Materials, Inc.

Unit 1: Two Vowels Together

Compound Words

> ℹ️ *Sunshine* is one word made up of two words: *sun* and *shine*. This is called a **compound word**.

1. Find the two words that make up these compound words.

	First Word	Second Word
airship	_____	_____
moonlight	_____	_____
overcoat	_____	_____
oatmeal	_____	_____
mainland	_____	_____
overload	_____	_____
mailman	_____	_____
airsick	_____	_____

2. Use the words from above to complete the following sentences.

   a. A _____ delivers letters and parcels.

   b. In an airplane they give you a brown paper bag just in case you become _____.

   c. At night, the explorer relied on_____ to see the path.

   d. The Zeppelin was the first _____.

   e. I had _____ and orange juice for breakfast today.

© Teacher Created Materials, Inc.

Unit 1: Two Vowels Together

Two-Vowel Poetry

Read the words then use them to complete each line of the poems.

1. | May — Saturday — play — holiday |

   It rains all day on _____

   When we have time to _____.

   I wait for the upcoming _____

   Coming up in the month of _____.

2. | domain — aim — plain — explain |

   Daisy the maid was oh so _____

   But to gain a husband was her _____.

   When the repairman came to her _____

   His fate was set. Need I _____?

3. | delay — say — away — yesterday |

   I say, I say, I _____,

   Did you hear about the man who got _____?

   We informed the police without _____

   Well, they finally caught him _____.

#3240 BBLS—Book 3: Vowel Sounds © Teacher Created Materials, Inc.

Unit 1: Two Vowels Together

Unit 1 Word List

Say the sound of the underlined vowels, and then say the words. (Read the words from left to right across the page.) How many words can you read in one minute?

season	cocoa	contain	detail
Friday	increase	treatment	charcoal
reveal	essay	explain	acquaint
repeat	appeal	complaint	dismay
teacher	peanut	display	decay
crayon	railway	decrease	gearbox
relay	defeat	beneath	oatmeal
teapot	reseal	ailment	reload
beaten	eager	restraint	mislaid
overcoat	ideal	anyway	astray
disease	repair	detain	domain
easel	beaker	raisin	obtain
ashtray	array	mayor	dearest
mailed	preacher	retail	peacock
repeat	prayer	loaded	tailor

Unit 2: Vowels and Word Endings

Using "y" as a Vowel

> **i** The letter *y* is a consonant when it is at the beginning of a word or syllable (for example, the word *yes*). Otherwise, it acts like the vowel *i*.
>
> The letter *y* can sound like:
> - the long sound /i/ as in *fly*
> - the long sound /e/ as in *baby*
> - the short sound /i/ as in *crystal*

1. Say and combine the syllables to make a word. Then look, say, listen, cover, write, and check!

hun	gry	_____	sun	ny	_____
hap	py	_____	emp	ty	_____
tren	dy	_____	pen	ny	_____
sup	ply	_____	re	ply	_____

2. Divide the following words into syllables (beats). Find the vowels. (Remember that *y* is acting as a vowel.) Divide the word between the consonants. Beware of blends!

	1st beat	2nd beat	Write the Word
twenty	_____	_____	_____
sticky	_____	_____	_____
comply	_____	_____	_____
angry	_____	_____	_____
mystic	_____	_____	_____
symptom	_____	_____	_____
empty	_____	_____	_____

Unit 2: Vowels and Word Endings

The Suffixes "ly" and "ty"

1. Read the word then add the suffix *ly*. Read the new word, then look, say, listen, cover, write, and check!

   bad____ _____   sick____ _____

   glad____ _____   like____ _____

   name____ _____   late____ _____

   lone____ _____   wide____ _____

2. Add *ty* or *ly* to the words to complete the sentences.

   a. You must arrive prompt____ at 7 P.M.

   b. Jenny is a very love____ girl.

   c. You must always put safe____ first.

   d. Grandma will be six____ in June.

   e. The robins fly swift____ over the hill.

   f. A scoop of ice cream can cost over nine____ cents.

   g. My dress is complete____ black.

   h. Sometimes I get very sad and lone____.

3. Find the base (root) word by taking off the suffix *ty* or *ly*.

   dimly _____   oddly _____

   sadly _____   seventy _____

   mostly _____   suddenly _____

   softly _____   safely _____

   quickly _____   flatly _____

   safety _____   sixty _____

© Teacher Created Materials, Inc. 19 #3240 BBLS—Book 3: Vowel Sounds

Unit 2: Vowels and Word Endings

Adding "es" and "ing"

> **i** When you want to add an ending to a word that ends in *y*, look at the letter before the *y*.
>
> - If there is a vowel before the *y*, just add the ending.
>   *Example:* say → saying
> - If there is a consonant before the *y*, change the *y* to *i* before adding the ending. *Example:* baby → babies
> - If the ending begins with *i* or a consonant then leave the *y* and add the ending. *Example:* cry → crying

1. Read the word, change the *y* to *i* and add *es*. Cover, then write the new word.

Word	Change the *y* to *i* and add *es*.	Cover, write, and check.
cry		
try		
fly		
carry		
hanky		
poppy		

2. Add *ing* to the following words. Then rewrite the entire word.

hurry_____   _____

study_____   _____

play_____   _____

stay_____   _____

worry_____   _____

obey_____   _____

Unit 2: Vowels and Word Endings

Making "y" Words Plural

> **i** **r** Words ending in *y* are also different when they are made plural (more than one).
>
> Look at the letter before the *y*.
> - If there is a vowel before the *y*, just add the ending *s*.
>   *Example:* monkey → monkeys
> - If there is a consonant before the *y*, change the *y* to *i* and add *es*.
>   *Example:* lady → ladies

1. Make these words plural (more than one).

   puppy _____   baby   _____

   pony   _____   lady   _____

   penny _____   doggy _____

   donkey _____   monkey _____

2. Make a new word by adding one of the suffixes *ing*, *er*, *ness*, or *est* to each of the following words. (Remember: if the suffix begins with a consonant or *i*, do not change the *y*.) Don't write the same word twice.

   worry _____   funny _____

   hurry _____   vary   _____

   merry _____   funny _____

   dusty _____   copy   _____

   dry   _____   dry   _____

   happy _____   happy _____

   messy _____   messy _____

   angry _____   lazy   _____

   empty _____   hungry _____

Unit 2: Vowels and Word Endings

Words with "ight"

> **i** The rime pattern *igh* says /i/ as in *five*. The rime pattern *ight* is used in many words. Think of *nightlight*. It has the *ight* pattern twice!

1. Find eight words that have *ight* as their rime. Use the consonant and consonant blend lists to help you.

   _____ _____ _____ _____

   _____ _____ _____ _____

2. Choose the best word to complete the sentence then cross out the other words.

   a. The boys began **fight fights fighting** after the football match.

   b. The stage lights needed **bright brighten brightening** so the actors could be seen.

   c. King Arthur had many **night nights knights** who were mighty fighting men.

   d. The rubbish at the seaside is **sights sightly unsightly**. It blemishes the sandy beaches.

   e. The little baby was **fright frightened frights** of the dark.

3. Add one of the suffixes *ful*, *less*, *ly*, *en*, or *ness* to the words so each sentence makes sense.

   a. The dodo was a bird that could not fly. It was flight_____.

   b. The bright_____ of the light made my eyes sting.

   c. I felt slight_____ ill after being on the high roller coaster.

   d. Tight_____ the lid before the juice drips out.

   e. What a fright_____ mess in here. Get it cleaned up.

#3240 BBLS—Book 3: Vowel Sounds   22   © Teacher Created Materials, Inc.

Unit 2: Vowels and Word Endings

"y" Word Poetry

Read the words then use them to complete each line of the poems.

1. | trying — denying — frying — crying |

    There is no _____
    It is rather _____.
    When onions are _____
    You always end up _____.

2. | mummy — happiest — hungriest — tummy |

    The baby's not at his _____
    When he's at his _____.
    The emptier his _____
    The more he cries like a _____.

3. | funny — shy — why — sunny |

    On days that were hot and _____
    The clown didn't feel nearly as _____.
    He said the sun just made him _____.
    But what he couldn't say was _____.

Unit 2: Vowels and Word Endings

Unit 2 Word List

> Say the underlined sounds, and then say the words. Read the words from left to right across the page. How many words can you read in one minute?

hung<u>ry</u>	sto<u>ry</u>	sor<u>ry</u>	glo<u>ry</u>
h<u>igh</u>	s<u>igh</u>	th<u>igh</u>	l<u>igh</u>t
hur<u>ry</u>	pen<u>ny</u>	lone<u>ly</u>	mes<u>sy</u>
s<u>igh</u>t	br<u>igh</u>t	t<u>igh</u>ts	twil<u>igh</u>t
st<u>u</u>d<u>y</u>	for<u>ty</u>	<u>e</u>mpt<u>y</u>	twen<u>ty</u>
fort<u>night</u>	<u>ti</u>ghten	<u>u</u>pright	h<u>igh</u>er
sun<u>ny</u>	ang<u>ry</u>	<u>ty</u>rant	sy<u>ru</u>p
h<u>igh</u><u>est</u>	luck<u>y</u>	s<u>y</u>stem	cr<u>y</u>ptic
m<u>y</u>stic	ber<u>ry</u>	fif<u>ty</u>	cher<u>ry</u>
bad<u>ly</u>	smo<u>ky</u>	wind<u>y</u>	happ<u>y</u>
app<u>ly</u>	rep<u>ly</u>	st<u>y</u>le	sh<u>y</u>
styl<u>ish</u>	de<u>light</u>	sky<u>light</u>	eye<u>sight</u>
cr<u>ied</u>	carr<u>ied</u>	fr<u>ied</u>	tr<u>ied</u>
fl<u>igh</u>t	migh<u>ty</u>	sil<u>ly</u>	fright<u>en</u>
bl<u>igh</u>t	c<u>ry</u>stal	six<u>ty</u>	mer<u>ry</u>

Unit 3: "ew" and "oo"

Reading "ew" and "oo"

> **i** There are two ways of saying *oo*:
> - /u/ as in *foot*
> - /oo/ as in *boot* and new.
>   *Example:* I need a new *boot* for my *foot*.

1. Underline the *oo* and *ew* in these one-syllable words. Then look, say, listen, cover, write, and check, putting the word into the correct box below.

food	grew	look	few	wood
threw	loose	good	goose	stood
choose	tooth	wool	took	chew
soon	room	crew	cook	stew

/oo/ as in "boot"

_____ _____
_____ _____
_____ _____
_____ _____

/u/ as in "foot"

_____ _____
_____ _____
_____ _____
_____ _____

/oo/ as in "crew"

_____ _____
_____ _____
_____ _____

2. Add a different suffix to each word so it makes sense. Choose *er, less, y, ing, en,* or *ish*. Some will have more than one right answer.

room_____   sleep_____   tooth_____
cook_____   wood_____   look_____
fool_____   self_____   self_____
point_____   mood_____   sweep_____

© Teacher Created Materials, Inc. 25 #3240 BBLS—Book 3: Vowel Sounds

Unit 3: "ew" and "oo"

Writing with "ew" and "oo"

1. Complete the sentences using your own words.

    a. Have you _____ my new _____?

    b. The crew _____ were pulling _____.

    c. I knew _____ so I _____.

    d. I threw _____ so hard that it _____.

    e. You must not chew _____, otherwise you'll _____.

    f. There are a few _____. Would you like _____?

    g. If I could choose my _____ I would _____.

2. Underline the *oo* in these two-syllable words. Then look, say, listen, cover, write, and check!

gloom	y	_____
bab	oon	_____
tat	too	_____
mon	soon	_____
mush	room	_____
poo	dle	_____
noo	dles	_____
bal	loons	_____
bas	soon	_____
coc	oon	_____
pre	school	_____
fool	ish	_____
car	toon	_____

Unit 3: "ew" and "oo"

Two-Syllable "oo" Words

1. Match the syllables to make a real word.

a.

bal	oon	_____
lag	room	_____
mon	phoon	_____
soo	ner	_____
mush	dle	_____
poo	soon	_____
ty	loon	_____

b.

roo	loo	_____
ig	oon	_____
sal	lish	_____
mar	toon	_____
foo	soon	_____
car	oon	_____
bas	ster	_____

2. Mark the vowels and consonants and find where each word is divided into syllables. (Remember: start from the first vowel.) Write the syllables on the lines.

	1st	2nd		1st	2nd
balloon	_____	_____	voodoo	_____	_____
shampoo	_____	_____	lagoon	_____	_____
igloo	_____	_____	mushroom	_____	_____
cocoon	_____	_____	toothache	_____	_____
noodle	_____	_____	baboon	_____	_____
platoon	_____	_____	festoon	_____	_____
typhoon	_____	_____	saloon	_____	_____
poodle	_____	_____	cartoon	_____	_____

© Teacher Created Materials, Inc. #3240 BBLS—Book 3: Vowel Sounds

Unit 3: "ew" and "oo"

More "oo," "ew," and "ui"

1. As you read the story, underline the words that contain *oo* or *ew*. Write your own ending for the story.

   It was late afternoon when my brother, the fool, threw the boomerang. It should have curved back, but it didn't. Just like a new harpoon, it hit the kangaroo between the eyes. The kangaroo looked up and zoomed towards us like a steam train. He looked like Road Runner, the cartoon character. Doom was near! I didn't bother to rinse the shampoo from my hair. I grabbed the packet of macaroons from the table and threw them in his path, hoping he would stop to chew them. He _____

   _____

   _____

   > **i** The vowels *ui* together say /oo/ as in *boot*.

2. In the following words *ui* says /oo/ as in *boot*. Practice reading these words and trace over each word three times. Then look, say, listen, cover, write, and check!

   fruit _____   suit _____   juice _____

   bruise _____   cruise _____ recruit _____

3. Use the words above to complete the sentences.

   a. The waiter spilled the _____ _____ down the front of my _____.

   b. I got a _____ on my arm when the _____ ship banged into the rocks.

Unit 3: "ew" and "oo"

"ew" and "oo" Poetry

1. | hero — moon — soon — zero |

   The rocket will set off _____

   On its final flight to the _____.

   The astronaut will be a _____

   Five, four, three, two, one, _____.

2. | chew — crew — barbecue — avenue |

   If you continue up the _____

   You'll catch the scent of a _____.

   Just go inside and say hello to the _____.

   There's plenty of food to bite and _____.

3. | spoon — moon — buffoon — afternoon |

   There was a silly _____

   Who wanted to fly to the _____.

   Except he was traveling by _____,

   And he fell back to Earth by _____.

Unit 3: "ew" and "oo"

Unit 3 Word List

Say the underlined sounds. Then practice reading and spelling the words. Read across the page from left to right. How many words can you read in one minute?

n<u>ew</u>	f<u>ew</u>	d<u>ew</u>	st<u>ew</u>
cr<u>ew</u>	bl<u>ew</u>	g<u>oo</u>d	b<u>oo</u>k
c<u>oo</u>k	l<u>oo</u>k	t<u>oo</u>k	st<u>oo</u>d
br<u>ew</u>	dr<u>ew</u>	ch<u>ew</u>	fl<u>ew</u>
gr<u>ew</u>	sl<u>ew</u>	f<u>oo</u>d	dr<u>oo</u>p
d<u>oo</u>m	m<u>oo</u>n	p<u>oo</u>l	r<u>oo</u>m
scr<u>ew</u>	thr<u>ew</u>	kn<u>ew</u>	st<u>ew</u>
shr<u>ew</u>d	cash<u>ew</u>	s<u>oo</u>n	ch<u>oo</u>se
sch<u>oo</u>l	sc<u>oo</u>ter	ball<u>oo</u>n	f<u>oo</u>lish
fr<u>ui</u>t	s<u>ui</u>t	j<u>ui</u>ce	cr<u>ui</u>se
br<u>ui</u>se	Hebr<u>ew</u>	cr<u>ew</u>cut	corkscr<u>ew</u>
withdr<u>ew</u>	m<u>oo</u>dy	tatt<u>oo</u>	p<u>oo</u>dle
mons<u>oo</u>n	sal<u>oo</u>n	fest<u>oo</u>n	bass<u>oo</u>n
mar<u>oo</u>n	harp<u>oo</u>n	plat<u>oo</u>n	mushr<u>oo</u>m
igl<u>oo</u>	vood<u>oo</u>	cart<u>oo</u>n	typh<u>oo</u>n

Unit 4: "ou"/"ow" and "oi"/"oy"

Words with "ou" and "ow"

> **i** The vowels *ou* and *ow* stay together in one syllable and say /ow/ as in *cow*.
>
> *Example:* Do not *shout* at that *cow*.

1. Add *ou* or *ow* to the following letters to make real words. Make sure they look right. Then look, say, listen, cover, write, and check!

   c____   _____   ____t   _____

   l____   _____   br____   _____

   f____nd _____   h____   _____

   r____   _____   s____   _____

   n____   _____   ab____t   _____

   r____nd _____   m____th   _____

   v____   _____   tr____sers _____

   ar____nd _____   acc____nt _____

   m____se _____   h____se   _____

2. Write down words that rhyme with the words below.

sound	shout	now

Unit 4: "ou"/"ow" and "oi"/"oy"

More Words with "ou" and "ow"

> **i** The letters *ow* are found in the middle of a word before *i*, *n*, and *er*.

1. Draw a line from the consonants to the rimes to make words. Then write the words on the blank lines. The first one is done for you.

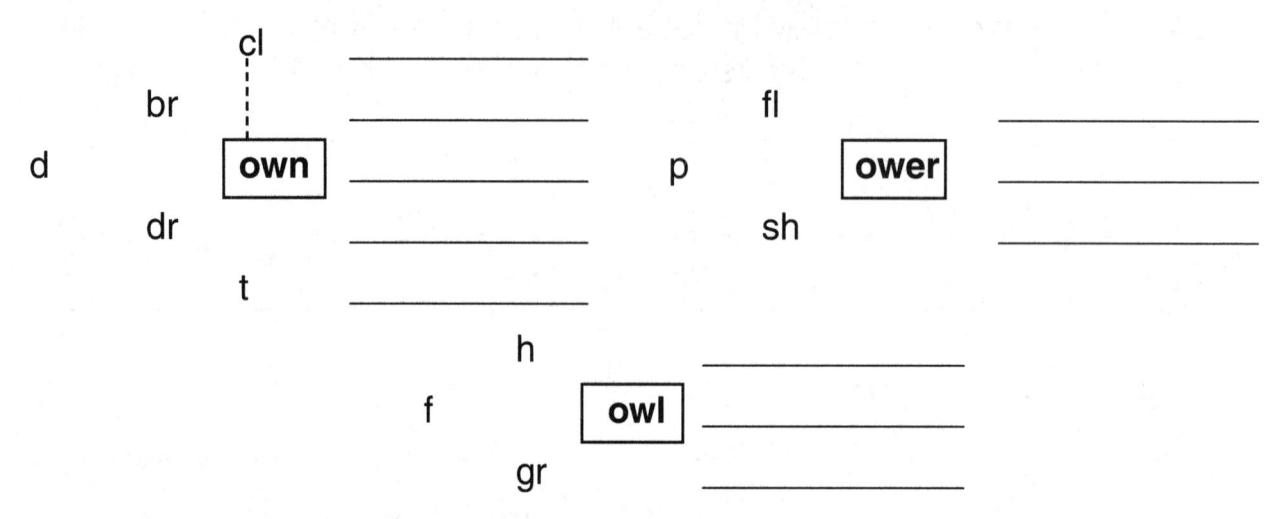

   cl _____
   br _____   fl _____
   d | own | _____   p | ower | _____
   dr _____   sh _____
   t   _____

                              h   _____
                          f | owl | _____
                              gr _____

2. Add the endings *ing* and *ed* to the following words. Then use one of the words to complete the sentence.

	Add *ing*.	**Add *ed*.**

   a. shout _____   _____
      The man was _____ at me to stop.

   b. sound _____   _____
      The pop music _____ very loud and deafened me.

   c. cloud _____   _____
      The sky was _____ over and it began to rain.

   d. scowl _____   _____
      The bank robber _____ at the cashier.

   e. shower _____   _____
      We take turns getting _____ every morning.

   f. allow _____   _____
      I was never _____ to chew gum in school.

#3240 BBLS—Book 3: Vowel Sounds © Teacher Created Materials, Inc.

Unit 4: "ou"/"ow" and "oi"/"oy"

Words with "oi" and "oy"

> **i** The letters *oi* and *oy* stay together in one syllable and say /oy/ as in *boy*.
> *Example:* The *boy points*.
> (Note: The letters *oi* are never found at the end of a word.)

1. Add the vowel pattern *oi* or *oy* to complete these one-syllable words. Make sure they look right. Then look, say, listen, cover, write, and check!

   s____   _____   b____l   _____

   c____l   _____   j____   _____

   j____nt _____   m____st   _____

   b____   _____   j____n   _____

   sp____l _____   t____   _____

   n____se _____   p____nt   _____

   ch____ce _____   v____ce   _____

2. Use the words above to complete these sentences.

   a. The _____ was making too much _____ with the trumpet.

   b. The tissue was _____ after wiping up the spilled _____ milk.

   c. It is a _____ to listen to a beautiful singing _____.

   d. If you _____ cabbage too long it will _____.

   e. "Please _____ to the candy of your _____," said the shopkeeper.

   f. We will have to use a _____ of wire to fix the _____.

Unit 4: "ou"/"ow" and "oi"/"oy"

More Words with "oi" and "oy"

1. Match the syllables to make a real word.

   a.
ap	joy	_____
em	noy	_____
an	point	_____
en	ploy	_____

   b.
de	joice	_____
a	coy	_____
re	void	_____
un	load	_____

2. Use the words above to complete the sentences.

   a. You _____ me by talking too much.

   b. I always try to _____ danger and housework!

   c. People _____ at the birth of a baby.

   d. The court will _____ a lawyer to the case.

   e. The noise was a _____ so the robbers could get into the bank.

   f. I _____ playing sports, especially soccer.

   g. The company was able to _____ fifteen hundred workers.

3. Read each syllable. Then rearrange them so they make a word you recognize.

   point – ap – dis   _____

   i – nois – ly   _____

   ment – ap – point   _____

   ploy – er – em   _____

   troy – des – er   _____

   ee – em – ploy   _____

Unit 4: "ou"/"ow" and "oi"/"oy"

Vowel Sound Poetry

Read the words in this box. Then use them to complete each line of the poems.

1. | out — sound — round — sprout |

   At dinner one night, I ate a bad _____.

   As soon as it went in, it wanted to come _____.

   It churned inside, going round and _____.

   It even caused a strange gurgling _____.

2. | enjoying — appointment — ointment — annoying |

   The dance I was _____

   When I tripped, which was _____.

   Then I had to make an _____

   At the doctors for some _____.

3. | loyal — flower — royal — flour |

   The king, who was quite _____

   Asked the baker, who was very _____

   To bake him a cake of sugar and _____

   And decorated with the petals of a _____.

© Teacher Created Materials, Inc.   35   #3240 BBLS—Book 3: Vowel Sounds

Unit 4: "ou"/"ow" and "oi"/"oy"

Unit 4 Word List

Say the underlined sounds. Then practice reading and spelling the words. Read across the page from left to right. How many words can you read in one minute?

point	hoist	moist	join
out	foul	loud	our
boy	joy	enjoy	annoy
crowd	frown	town	gown
cloud	house	count	ounce
growl	scowl	flower	drowsy
destroy	loyal	employ	alloy
mouth	bounce	shout	round
noise	choice	voice	toilet
lounge	scrounge	blouse	county
allow	coward	however	power
powder	shower	vowel	disallow
avoid	turquoise	appoint	exploit
account	announce	boundary	council
moisten	tabloid	recoil	devoid

Unit 5: Three-Syllable Vowel Sounds

Three-Syllable Words

> ℹ️ Three-syllable words have three beats when you say them, so they can be split into three parts. There is a vowel sound in every beat.

1. Say each syllable and combine them to make a word. Then look, say, listen, cover, write, and check!

   No•vem•ber _____

   Oc•to•ber _____

   re•mem•ber _____

   bas•ket•ball _____

   la•bor•er _____

   ro•man•tic _____

   e•quip•ment _____

   ver•tic•al _____

2. Read the words again. Make sure you know what they all mean.

3. Write each syllable of the words above under the correct type of syllable.

Open syllable (ends in vowel)	Vowel + r syllable (ends with vowel + r)	Closed syllable (ends in consonant)
_____	_____	_____ _____
_____	_____	_____ _____
_____	_____	_____ _____
_____	_____	_____ _____
_____	_____	_____ _____

© Teacher Created Materials, Inc.   37   #3240 BBLS—Book 3: Vowel Sounds

Unit 5: Three-Syllable Vowel Sounds

Dividing Three Syllables

Mark the vowels first, then mark the consonants and decide where to split the words into syllables (beats).

VC Pattern	1st Beat	2nd Beat	3rd Beat	Cover, Write, and Check
fantastic				
estimate				
vitamins				
illustrate				
pendulum				
hexagon				
consider				
parallel				
capital				
positive				
infantile				
badminton				
components				
kilogram				
examine				
unison				
negative				

Read the words again. Make sure you know the meaning of all these words. Look in a dictionary if you don't.

#3240 BBLS—Book 3: Vowel Sounds   38   © Teacher Created Materials, Inc.

Unit 5: Three-Syllable Vowel Sounds

Using Three-Syllable Words

1. Read the words. They are split up into their syllables.

   un•der•stand   im•por•tant   o•ver•come

   dis•em•bark   ar•gu•ment   im•mor•tal

   im•pro•vise   in•ter•act   dif•fer•ent

   im•pro•vise   in•ter•est   sep•ar•ate

2. Use the words above to complete the sentences below. Use a dictionary to help you. The sentences must make sense.

   a. My hobby and _____ is collecting shells.

   b. I shall have to _____ you two if you do not stop talking when I am trying to give a lesson.

   c. The movie had no script. The actors were asked to _____ their roles.

   d. We had to _____ from the ship at 10 o'clock.

   e. The old lady died because she had been _____ by the fumes from the fire.

   f. My black socks are _____ than your white socks.

   g. The boy was _____ to get his bike back before his mom found that it was missing.

   h. We had an _____ about who was going to wash up first.

   i. Children need to learn how to _____ with others.

   j. 007 James Bond seems _____. He never dies in his films.

   k. It is _____ that you _____ what I am saying.

© Teacher Created Materials, Inc.   39   #3240 BBLS—Book 3: Vowel Sounds

Unit 5: Three-Syllable Vowel Sounds

Understanding Three-Syllable Words

1. Match the words to their meanings. You may need to use a dictionary.

a.

Word	Meaning
negative	make up for
estimate	1,000 grams
components	guess
kilogram	minus
compensate	parts

b.

Word	Meaning
vitamins	outside something
external	straight up
internal	inspect
vertical	goodness in food
examine	inside something

2. Choose one of the words above to complete the following sentences.

   a. A _____ bag of sugar holds the same as 1,000 grams.

   b. -3 is a _____ number.

   c. A _____ line goes up and down.

   d. Please _____ the height of the room in feet.

   e. The electrical _____ in a computer are very small.

   f. Sun screen is for _____ use only.

   g. I want you to _____ me for my pen that you lost.

   h. We should all eat fresh foods so we know we are getting the minerals and _____ we need.

   i. The heart is an _____ organ.

   j. _____ your change before leaving the shop, as mistakes cannot be rectified.

Unit 5: Three-Syllable Vowel Sounds

Three-Syllable Poetry

Read the words then use them to complete each line of the poems.

1. romantic — surprise — Atlantic — paradise

    It was very _____

    To cruise across the _____.

    It was a great _____

    To be a guest in _____.

2. do — regular — muscular — two

    If I want to make my body _____

    I have to keep my exercise _____.

    I must lose a pound or _____.

    Follow a diet is what I'll _____.

3. comical — monocle — bicycle — maniacal

    Some say he looks _____

    Pedaling so fast on his _____.

    Others say he's just _____

    Squinting through one large _____.

Unit 5: Three-Syllable Vowel Sounds

Unit 5 Word List

> Read the underlined syllables. Then read the words. (Remember to read from left to right across the page.) Make sure you know what each word means. How many words can you read in one minute?

uni<u>form</u>	p<u>o</u>pular	dev<u>e</u>lop	<u>p</u>rofessor
<u>ca</u>pital	<u>po</u>litics	hesit<u>ate</u>	re<u>ve</u>rsal
<u>p</u>arallel	prop<u>er</u>ties	parad<u>ise</u>	anim<u>al</u>
<u>ba</u>ritone	vis<u>i</u>tor	<u>ca</u>lendar	colle<u>c</u>tor
com<u>i</u>cal	simil<u>ar</u>	doc<u>u</u>ment	magni<u>tude</u>
edu<u>cate</u>	remem<u>ber</u>	<u>e</u>xternal	al<u>c</u>ohol
ar<u>ro</u>gant	<u>c</u>ompliment	in<u>te</u>rnal	diff<u>i</u>cult
<u>i</u>rritate	in<u>ti</u>mate	hos<u>p</u>ital	<u>i</u>nfantile
<u>en</u>velope	in<u>te</u>rfere	per<u>ma</u>nent	singu<u>lar</u>
al<u>ti</u>tude	custo<u>mer</u>	hurri<u>cane</u>	<u>A</u>tlantic
narra<u>tive</u>	sensi<u>tive</u>	<u>fa</u>ntastic	<u>in</u>tervene
ver<u>ti</u>cal	instruc<u>tor</u>	<u>c</u>onfiscate	tran<u>sis</u>tor
muscu<u>lar</u>	a<u>g</u>nostic	<u>e</u>stablish	can<u>di</u>date
atten<u>dant</u>	sudden<u>ly</u>	<u>b</u>adminton	<u>in</u>terval
thermo<u>stat</u>	<u>b</u>icycle	monu<u>ment</u>	musi<u>cal</u>

Student Target Sheets

✣ Completed Worksheets

After receiving marked worksheets, students can color in the appropriate square or squares on their sheet under "Completed Work." For example, if pages 12 and 18 have been completed, then the boxes relating to pages 12 and 18 are colored in. Marking should be strict. Students handing in incomplete pages should not be allowed to color in the target. This will encourage students to ask for help if they are having difficulties and will discourage sloppy work.

✣ Oral Assessment

While students are completing a task they can be checked for their understanding of the work that has been covered. The questions to be asked for each target follow these instructions. For any correct answer the appropriate rectangle should be colored in immediately on their Target Sheet.

Tutors can use their discretion as to how much help they give to students to enable them to complete a target. Help should be given in the form of modeling. The tutor completes an activity relating to the target question, then asks the student that same question. If the student is successful then he or she has completed that target and it may be colored in.

The tutor can use the information gained from the students' answers to find which areas need more attention and explanation. These may be addressed as a whole-class activity or with individual students.

✣ Reading Targets

The targets set for reading are based on speed and should be set according to the literacy level of the group or individual; and they must be attainable. It may be more appropriate just to record the number of words read in a certain time (e.g., 60 seconds) rather than give a definite speed for reading.

Pupils reading the word lists at home can keep an accurate record of their reading by filling in a graph (see Appendix 1). This will show a clear record of the increase in their speed of reading.

✣ Spelling Targets

The target words set for spelling should, if possible, be words the students will tend to use. The number of words given is at the discretion of the tutor.

✣ Appropriateness

The Student Target Sheets may not be suitable for those with very low literacy skills. It is left to the discretion of the tutor whether to use them or not.

Student Target Sheets

Tutor's Instructions for Student Target Sheet

page 12	What do you usually have to remember when two vowels follow one another in a word with more than one syllable? (*Keep the two vowels together in the same syllable.*)
page 12	What do you have to remember when you are splitting words up into syllables? (*There must be a vowel sound in every syllable.*)
page 18	If the letter "y" is at the beginning of a word how does it sound? (*like a consonant, as in the word "yes"*)
page 18	The letter "i" is never at the end of an English word. Which letter takes the place of the "i" sound at the end of a word? (*the letter "y"*)
page 18	How many sounds does the letter "y" have? (*four: /y/ as in "yes," long /e/ as in "baby," long /i/ as in "fly," short /i/ as in "crystal"*)
page 22	When you see the letters "igh" together in a word what sound do they give? (*long /i/ as in "five"*)
page 25	What two sounds can the letters "oo" say in a word? (*the /u/ sound, as in "foot"; and /oo/ as in "boot"*)
page 25	What does the "ew" say in the word "chew"? (*It says /oo/.*)
page 28	What does the "ui" say in the word "fruit"? (*It says /oo/.*)
page 31	When you see the vowels "ou" together in the middle of a word, what do they say? (*They say /ow/ as in "cow."*)
page 33	When you see the vowels "oi" together in the middle of a word, what do they say? (*They say /oy/ as in "boy."*)
page 37	How many vowel sounds will a three-syllable word have? (*three*)
page 37	How many beats has a three-syllable word? (*three*)

Student Target Sheets

Student Target Sheet

Name: _____ Date started: _____

Completed work	I know . . .	Reading	Spelling
Unit 1	**Two Vowels Together**	I can read _____ words in _____ seconds.	I can spell _____ out of _____.
page 12	to keep vowels that follow one another together in one syllable.		
page 12	there is a vowel sound in every syllable.		
Unit 2	**Vowels and Word Endings**	I can read _____ words in _____ seconds.	I can spell _____ out of _____.
page 18	that "y" is a consonant at the beginning of a word.		
page 18	that "y" replaces (i) at the end of a word.		
page 18	that "y" had four sounds.		
page 22	"igh" says (i) as in "five".		
Unit 3	**"ew" and "oo"**	I can read _____ words in _____ seconds.	I can spell _____ out of _____.
page 25	that "oo" has two sounds – (u) as in "foot" and)oo) as in "boot".		
page 25	"ew" says (oo) as in "boot".		
page 28	that the vowels "ui" together say the sound (oo) as in "boot".		
Unit 4	**"ou"/"ow" and "oi"/"oy"**	I can read _____ words in _____ seconds.	I can spell _____ out of _____.
page 31	"ou" says (ow) as in "cow" and is never found at the end of a word.		
page 33	"oi" says (oy) as in "boy" and is never found at the end of a word.		
Unit 5	**Three-Syllable Vowel Sounds**	I can read _____ words in _____ seconds.	I can spell _____ out of _____.
page 37	that three-syllable words have three vowel sounds.		
page 37	that three-syllable words have three beats.		

© Teacher Created Materials, Inc. #3240 BBLS—Book 3: Vowel Sounds

Student Target Sheets

CERTIFICATE OF ACHIEVEMENT

Awarded to

For successfully completing Units 1–5 of the Building Basic Literacy Skills program

_____
Signature

_____
Date

Appendix 1

Graph of Reading Speed

Ask the students to read the Word List on the last page of the unit being worked on every day. They should count the number of words read in one minute and put a mark on the graph for that unit to indicate this number. You may need to provide the student with several copies of the graph for each unit, depending on the number of sessions taken to complete it.

The completed graphs will give a clear indication of progress and will motivate the students. It is important to encourage the students to become familiar with reading accurately under pressure as this is what is expected of them during their internal and external exams.

Graph of Words Read in One Minute

Name: Jane Lee   Unit: 1

Date	9/30	10/6	10/13	10/20	10/27
Words read	27	30	29	36	35

© Teacher Created Materials, Inc.   47   #3240 BBLS—Book 3: Vowel Sounds

Appendix 1

Graph of Words Read in One Minute

Name: _____ Unit: _____

60													
59													
58													
57													
56													
55													
54													
53													
52													
51													
50													
49													
48													
47													
46													
45													
44													
43													
42													
41													
40													
39													
38													
37													
36													
35													
34													
33													
32													
31													
30													
29													
28													
27													
26													
25													
24													
23													
22													
21													
20													
19													
18													
17													
16													
15													
14													
13													
12													
11													
10													
9													
8													
7													
6													
5													
4													
3													
2													
1													
Date:													

#3240 BBLS—Book 3: Vowel Sounds © Teacher Created Materials, Inc.

Appendix 2

The "Self Voice" Method

The "self voice" is likened to the voice we hear inside our heads when we are concentrating intently on information given verbally: we sub-vocalize what we hear. We can try to recreate this "concentration" by the students using a tape recorder to record themselves reading and then listening to the tape.

Any spelling that is causing a problem can be recorded onto tape and then listened to. The procedure for this is as follows:

1. The words to learn are identified from the word lists and errors found in class work. (The number of spelling words given will depend on the literacy level of each student.)

2. The student reads the word to the tutor. The tutor ensures that the pronunciation of the word is correct.

3. The student reads the whole word onto tape, then reads the name of each letter that makes up the word while tracing over the word with a pen. (Count to three silently while the tape is on record between each word to ensure that the student can easily recognize the end of each word.)

4. The tape is rewound.

5. The student listens to a word and the letter names; he or she then pauses the tape and writes down the spelling of the word. All the words are listened to and written down in this way.

It is important to encourage the student to wait until the end of the naming of the letters of a word before he or she writes down the letters. This brings in a memory element to the procedure.

Students can listen to the tape as many times as they wish. They may also record just the whole word on the reverse side of the tape and then check their own spelling knowledge if they wish to.

Be aware that a student may mix up the letter names with the incorrect shapes. To check this, ask the student to write down the shapes of the letters as you recite the letter names from A to Z.

Appendix 3

Phonic Spell Checks

A check of non-real words can be made on the phonic knowledge of students by giving them spell checks. The words are non-real so the students will have to use their knowledge of phonics to attempt to spell the words (auditory to orthographic).

The students can also be asked to read the words to check their visual phonetic knowledge.

✣ **Phonic Spell Check for Short Vowels and Single Consonants**

The words below and on page 51 can be photocopied onto cardstock to make word cards. After working through Unit 1, ask each student to read these **cvc** words. Use the "Phonic Checklist" (Appendix 4, page 52) to keep a record of sounds known.

tud	fug
yem	quot
hul	bup

#3240 BBLS—Book 3: Vowel Sounds © Teacher Created Materials, Inc.

Appendix 3

Phonic Spell Checks (cont.)

nal	cas
pob	sut
gax	kef
noz	wiv
mib	maz
ris	vek

Appendix 4

Phonic Checklist

After giving the non-real word spell check, mark on the checklist all of the single consonants and vowels the student has successfully identified. Sound cards should be made of any letters not known by the student. (See Appendix 6 on page 57.)

Appendix 4

Phonic Checklist (cont.)

Name:_____

	Spelled	Read
a		
b		
c		
d		
e		
f		
g		
h		
i		
j		
k		
l		
m		
n		
o		
p		
qu		
r		
s		
t		
u		
v		
w		

	Spelled	Read
x		
y		
z		
bl		
cl		
fl		
gl		
pl		
sl		
br		
cr		
dr		
fr		
gr		
pr		
tr		
sp		
sc		
sk		
sm		
sn		
sw		
tw		

	Spelled	Read
ch		
sh		
th		
nh		
ct		
nt		
lf		
ck		
ss		
ft		
ld		
lk		
pt		
xt		
mp		
sk		
st		
lp		
sp		
nd		
lt		
lm		
nk		

Date started: _____   Date completed: _____

© Teacher Created Materials, Inc.   53   #3240 BBLS—Book 3: Vowel Sounds

Appendix 5

Phonic Spell Check for Consonant Blends

After Unit 3, a non-real word spell check should be given to identify the consonant blends the student knows. The words that follow can be photocopied onto card to make word cards. The check should be given in at least two parts: first the initial blends and then the final blends. Mark the blends known on the Phonic Checklist. Sound cards can be made of those blends not mastered. (See Appendix 6.)

Appendix 5

Initial Blends

slat	smoc	twil	prip	swul
frat	grop	flig	triv	snex
glib	scun	brug	dreb	crit
spup	tham	sked	shum	thap
clem	blag	pleb	skib	chan

Appendix 5

Final Blends

zeng	deft	dask	folm	gesh
tross	himp	palt	tock	pumb
tuxt	wend	gilf	upt	lasm
cusp	ront	pelk	hulp	murf
tict	vald	zast	vank	yown

Appendix 6

Sound Cards

To become accurate readers and spellers, students generally need to know the sound each letter or letter blend represents. Each letter has a shape (symbol) that represents a particular sound. Sound cards can be used to teach students sound-symbol correspondence and should be practiced every day until sound-symbol correspondences are known.

The words that follow can be photocopied onto cardstock and cut into sound cards. If the students cannot read the words then a picture clue can be drawn to represent each word.

The student holds the cards, then does the following:

1. says the word on the card (a picture may be needed as a clue to the word)

    For example:

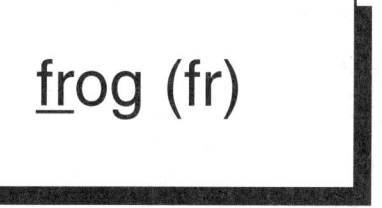

    frog (fr)

2. listens for the sound of the letters that are underlined

3. says the sound the underlined letters make (the phonetic sound of these letters is given in brackets).

Model this procedure so the students know what is expected of them.

To check that the students can recognize the sound that a symbol represents (grapheme to phoneme) it is useful to write the letter being practiced on the back of each sound card. Ask the student to read the letter side of the sound cards only and to say the sound of the letter.

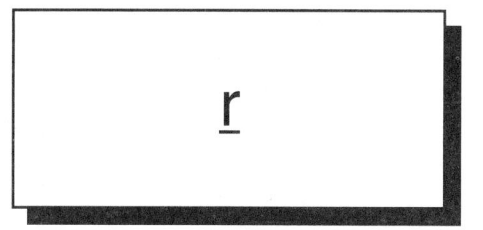

For example:

r   rabbit (r)

© Teacher Created Materials, Inc.   #3240 BBLS—Book 3: Vowel Sounds

Appendix 6

Sound Cards *(cont.)*

To check that the student knows sound-symbol correspondence (phoneme to grapheme):

1. Read the word on each sound card and isolate the sound of the underlined letters.

2. Ask the student to write down the symbols that represent each sound.

3. Check that the symbols are correct for each sound.

Keep a check on progress by recording all of the sound-symbol correspondences the students have learned on the Phonic Checklist (see Appendix 4).

Up to ten sound cards may be given each week, depending on the student's ability. As each sound card is learned, another sound card can be included to make up the number.

Students may know many of the sounds. To check which they know, either the non-real word check can be given (see Appendix 5) or follow this procedure:

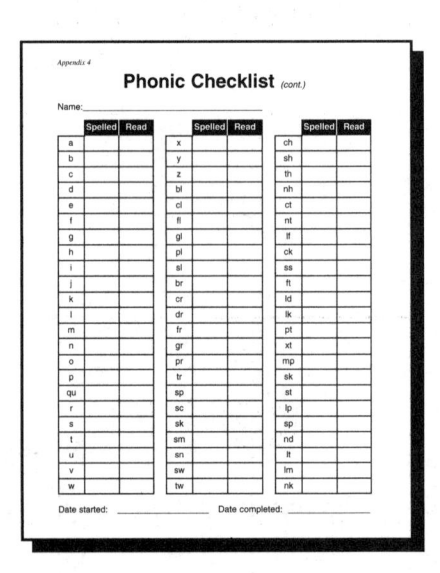

1. Read through the sound cards once with the student.

2. Ensure that the student cannot see the cards, then ask him or her to write down the symbols that represent each sound.

3. Record all sound-symbol correspondence known on the Phonic Checklist.

(The sound cards can be photocopied onto cards. It is useful to edge the cards that represent the vowels with a color to make them stand out from the consonants and blends.)

Sound Cards for Single Consonants and Vowel Sounds

apple (a)	egg (e)	Indian (i)
orange (o)	umbrella (u)	bat (b)
cat (k)	dog (d)	fish (f)
goat (g)	house (h)	jacket (j)
kite (k)	lemon (l)	mouse (m)
neck (n)	peg (p)	zebra (z)
rabbit (r)	socks (s)	table (t)
van (v)	window (w)	yellow (y)

Appendix 6

Sound Cards for Consonant Blends at the Beginning of Words

thumb (th)	queen (kw)	black (bl)
clown (kl)	flag (fl)	frame (fr)
glove (gl)	plant (pl)	slide (sl)
brown (br)	crab (kr)	drum (dr)
frog (fr)	grapes (gr)	prop (pr)
train (tr)	scarf (sk)	smoke (sm)
snake (sn)	sweets (sw)	twins (tw)
skirt (sk)	spider (sp)	steps (st)

Sound Cards Containing Initial and Final Consonant Blends

wo**rk** (rk)	**ch**ips (ch)	**sh**op (sh)
de**sk** (sk)	ma**tch** (ch)	ne**st** (st)
wa**sh** (sh)	be**lt** (lt)	mi**lk** (lk)
a**ct** (kt)	le**ft** (ft)	te**nt** (nt)
ha**nd** (nd)	si**nk** (nk)	la**mp** (mp)
clo**ck** (k)	ri**ng** (ng)	**spl**inter (spl)
spring (spr)	**str**ing (str)	**scr**ipt (skr)
shrink (shr)	**thr**ee (thr)	**squ**id (skw)

Appendix 7

Cards for Word Games

As the *Building Basic Literacy Skills* is phonic-based, students should, in addition, have practice reading the words as whole words.

The pages that follow can be enlarged and photocopied onto cards to make word cards for games that supplement the work of each unit. Playing games is challenging, involves unconscious learning, and is enjoyed by the students. Students can also make their own word cards to take home and so reinforce the work learned in class.

One set of each reading card can be used for:

- reading through at speed.
- sorting the cards into families. The students identify the families.

Also, the cards can be used for the following card games:

⇒ **Grab!**

The tutor holds a card up for two seconds only. The players have to write the word down correctly. One point is given for each correct spelling.

⇒ **Matching Families**

The family might be:

- matching a singular word with its plural: e.g., *cat* with *cats*
- matching a base word with two different endings: e.g., *bat*, *batted*, and *batting*

In both Matching Families games, five or seven cards are dealt out to each player and the extra cards placed in the center of the table. The top card is turned face up from this pack and placed alongside the pack that is face down to start a second pack of cards.

The first player selects the upturned card if it matches his or her "hand." If not, the player selects a card from the pack that is face down. He or she drops an unwanted card and places it face up on the pile. Players must always have the original number of cards in their hand except for the winning card. The first player to find a matching family wins the game.

Appendix 7

Cards for Word Games *(cont.)*

⇒ **Robbers**

A number of cards are placed face up on the table by the dealer. The cards are read by the player. The dealer removes one card while the player is not looking. How many cards can the player remember?

⇒ **Spelling Dice**

The speller throws the dice. The reader counts the number of cards out onto the table, except for the card indicated by the dice number—this is read out to the speller. The speller has to spell the word correctly, and keeps the card if he or she is correct. If he or she spells it incorrectly, then the reader returns the card to the pile. They swap over, and the speller becomes the reader. The student with the most cards at the end of the game wins.

Two of the same cards can be copied and used for:

⇒ **Snap**

To play this game shuffle the word cards. Deal out all the cards one at a time to each player. Each player keeps his or her cards face down in front of them in a pile. Each time the player's turn comes up, the player turns a card from his or her pile face up, reads the word, and forms a new pile in front of the others.

When two cards of the same word are turned up and read, the first player who has either card and calls "Snap" wins the matched pair. The winner places the cards won under his or her main face-down pile.

If both players call "Snap" at the same time, both cards are placed into a pile in the middle of the table. The next player who turns up a card matching those in the pile may call "Snap" and win the cards in the pile.

Anyone calling "Snap" in error places his or her face up cards in the pool. When a player loses all his or her cards, he or she is out of the game. The player who ends up with all the cards wins the game.

⇒ **Concentration**

Place the cards face down on the table. Players alternate turning over two cards. The cards must be read aloud. The object of the game is to find like or corresponding pairs. A player finding a pair can have another go. This game develops the students' concentration and memory.

Unit 1: Two Vowels Together

season	beaten	appeal
Friday	overcoat	peanut
reveal	disease	railway
repeat	easel	defeat
teacher	ashtray	raisin
crayon	cocoa	eager
relay	increase	ideal
teapot	essay	beaker

Unit 1: Two Vowels Together (cont.)

array	ailment	dismay
contain	restraint	decay
treatment	anyway	oatmeal
explain	detain	reload
complaint	mayor	astray
display	detail	domain
decrease	charcoal	obtain
beneath	acquaint	dearest

Appendix 7

Unit 2: "y" or "igh" as a Vowel

hungry	badly	tighten
high	apply	angry
hurry	stylish	lucky
sight	story	berry
study	sigh	smoky
sunny	penny	reply
highest	bright	sorry
mystic	forty	delight

Unit 2: "y" or "igh" as a Vowel (cont.)

thigh	system	twenty
lonely	windy	higher
tight	style	cryptic
fifty	glory	syrup
sixty	light	cherry
empty	messy	happy
upright	night	shy
tyrant	twilight	eyesight

Appendix 7

Unit 3: The /oo/ Sound

new	few	stew
crew	blew	grew
brew	drew	chew
knew	screw	shrewd
food	droop	moon
school	scooter	balloon
foolish	shampoo	moody
tattoo	afternoon	mushroom

Unit 4: Words with "ou" or "ow"

out	foul	loud
our	cloud	house
count	ounce	mouth
bounce	shout	round
lounge	blouse	county
account	vowel	council
fountain	announce	powder
thousand	scoundrel	boundary

Appendix 7

Unit 4: Words with "oi" or "oy"

coin	joint	spoil
point	hoist	moist
moisten	destroy	loyal
employ	alloy	noise
choice	voice	toilet
avoid	turquoise	tabloid
cuboid	exploit	thyroid
boycott	poison	devoid

Unit 5: Three-Syllable Words

uniform	popular	develop
professor	capital	hesitate
reversal	parallel	properties
paradise	animal	visitor
calendar	collector	comical
similar	document	magnitude
educate	remember	external
alcohol	arrogant	internal

Unit 5: Three-Syllable Words (cont.)

difficult	irritate	intimate
hospital	infantile	envelope
interfere	permanent	singular
altitude	customer	hurricane
fantastic	intervene	vertical
instructor	confiscate	transistor
muscular	establish	candidate
attendant	musical	descriptive

Answer Key

The program is largely self-checking and typical answers for each page of instruction are located in the answer key along with direct points of guidance for the tutor.

Since the students are actively encouraged to take control of their own learning, it may be sensible for the tutor to allow them to mark and rate their own work. This may be monitored by encouraging students to exchange scripts to mark a partner's work. This will again involve reading and following instructions, and in itself may encourage the students to think more carefully about the patterns of letters within words.

Answer Key (cont.)

Page 12

Dividing Syllables

Unit 1: Two Vowels Together

To divide a word into syllables (beats):
- Find the vowels and mark them with the letter **v**.
- Mark the consonants between the vowels with the letter **c**.
- Split the word into two: **vc/cv**, **v/cv**, or **vc/v**.

1. Say the sound of the vowels and combine the syllables to make a word. Then look, say, listen, cover, write, and check!

a.
a	sleep	asleep
cray	on	crayon
de	cay	decay
re	veal	reveal
con	tain	contain

b.
com	plaint	complaint
re	peat	repeat
be	tween	between
un	load	unload
tea	cher	teacher

2. Keeping the two vowels together, divide the words into syllables. Then look, say, listen, cover, write, and check!

	1st beat	2nd beat	Write the Word
obtain	ob	tain	obtain
treatment	treat	ment	treatment
coffee	cof	fee	coffee
freedom	free	dom	freedom
beneath	be	neath	beneath
disease	dis	ease	disease
tweezers	twee	zers	tweezers
remain	re	main	remain

Page 13

Matching Syllables

Unit 1: Two Vowels Together

1. Match the syllables to make a real word.

Mon — cay — Monday
can — ish — canteen
de — day — decay
tea — teen — teacher
dis — leen — disease
six — cher — sixteen
squeam — teen — squeamish
Kath — ease — Kathleen

2. Use the words above in the blanks. Then complete the story in your own words.

Last __Monday__ we found some maggots in the school's water __canteen__. Someone had left meat to __decay__ on a plate near the canteen. The __teacher__ said if we had eaten the meat we would have gotten a __disease__. There were __sixteen__ maggots wriggling about. I felt a bit __squeamish__, but __Kathleen__ was sick on the spot! While the teacher was comforting her, Kevin picked up a maggot and put it _____.

Page 14

Using Two Vowels Together

Unit 1: Two Vowels Together

1. Cross out the incorrect words in the sentences.
   a. There are seven ~~day~~ days in a week.
   b. Tony ~~cheat cheats~~ cheated in last year's exams.
   c. "Your school report was very ~~please pleased~~ pleasing, Tim."
   d. My teeth are ~~decay decays~~ decaying because I eat too many sweets.
   e. When I go on vacation this summer, I am ~~stay stays~~ staying in a hotel.
   f. Why do I always have to repeat ~~repeats repeating~~ myself?
   g. The shop was ~~display displays~~ displaying a selection of toys.
   h. He ~~appeal appealed~~ appealing to his mom to let him watch the television program.

2. Complete these sentences using your own words.
   a. I am very pleased about _____ because I _____.
   b. The reason I am mad is because _____ and you _____.
   c. When you have measles you have _____ and sometimes you _____.
   d. My dream is to _____ so I _____.

Page 15

Compound Words

Unit 1: Two Vowels Together

Sunshine is one word made up of two words: *sun* and *shine*. This is called a **compound word**.

1. Find the two words that make up these compound words.

	First Word	Second Word
airship	air	ship
moonlight	moon	light
overcoat	over	coat
oatmeal	oat	meal
mainland	main	land
overload	over	load
mailman	mail	man
airsick	air	sick

2. Use the words from above to complete the following sentences.
   a. A __mailman__ delivers letters and parcels.
   b. In an airplane they give you a brown paper bag just in case you become __airsick__.
   c. At night, the explorer relied on __moonlight__ to see the path.
   d. The Zeppelin was the first __airship__.
   e. I had __oatmeal__ and orange juice for breakfast today.

Answer Key (cont.)

Page 16

Unit 1: Two Vowels Together

Two-Vowel Poetry

Read the words then use them to complete each line of the poems.

1. May — Saturday — play — holiday

   It rains all day on **Saturday**.
   When we have time to **play**.
   I wait for the upcoming **holiday**.
   Coming up in the month of **May**.

2. domain — aim — plain — explain

   Daisy the maid was oh so **plain**.
   But to gain a husband was her **aim**.
   When the repairman came to her **domain**.
   His fate was set. Need I **explain**?

3. delay — say — away — yesterday

   I say, I say, I **say**,
   Did you hear about the man who got **away**?
   We informed the police without **delay**.
   Well, they finally caught him **yesterday**.

Page 18

Unit 2: Vowels and Word Endings

Using "y" as a Vowel

The letter *y* is a consonant when it is at the beginning of a word or syllable (for example, the word *yes*). Otherwise, it acts like the vowel *i*.

The letter *y* can sound like:
- the long sound /i/ as in *fly*
- the long sound /e/ as in *baby*
- the short sound /i/ as in *crystal*

1. Say and combine the syllables to make a word. Then look, say, listen, cover, write, and check!

hun	gry	hungry	sun	ny	sunny
hap	py	happy	emp	ty	empty
tren	dy	trendy	pen	ny	penny
sup	ply	supply	re	ply	reply

2. Divide the following words into syllables (beats). Find the vowels. (Remember that y is acting as a vowel.) Divide the word between the consonants. Beware of blends!

	1st beat	2nd beat	Write the Word
twenty	twen	ty	twenty
sticky	stick	y	sticky
comply	com	ply	comply
angry	ang	ry	angry
mystic	mys	tic	mystic
symptom	symp	ton	sympton
empty	emp	ty	empty

Page 19

Unit 2: Vowels and Word Endings

The Suffixes "ly" and "ty"

1. Read the word then add the suffix *ly*. Read the new word, then look, say, listen, cover, write, and check!

bad_ly_	badly	sick_ly_	sickly
glad_ly_	gladly	like_ly_	likely
name_ly_	namely	late_ly_	lately
lone_ly_	lonely	wide_ly_	widely

2. Add *ty* or *ly* to the words to complete the sentences.

   a. You must arrive prompt_ly_ at 7 P.M.
   b. Jenny is a very love_ly_ girl.
   c. You must always put safe_ty_ first.
   d. Grandma will be six_ty_ in June.
   e. The robins fly swift_ly_ over the hill.
   f. A scoop of ice cream can cost over nine_ty_ cents.
   g. My dress is complete_ly_ black.
   h. Sometimes I get very sad and lone_ly_.

3. Find the base (root) word by taking off the suffix *ty* or *ly*.

dimly	dim	oddly	odd
sadly	sad	seventy	seven
mostly	most	suddenly	sudden
softly	soft	safely	safe
quickly	quick	flatly	flat
safety	safe	sixty	six

Page 20

Unit 2: Vowels and Word Endings

Adding "es" and "ing"

When you want to add an ending to a word that ends in *y*, look at the letter before the *y*.
- If there is a vowel before the *y*, just add the ending. *Example:* say → saying
- If there is a consonant before the *y*, change the *y* to *i* before adding the ending. *Example:* baby → babies
- If the ending begins with *i* or a consonant then leave the *y* and add the ending. *Example:* cry → crying

1. Read the word, change the *y* to *i* and add *es*. Cover, then write the new word.

Word	Change the *y* to *i* and add *es*.	Cover, write, and check.
cry	cries	cries
try	tries	tries
fly	flies	flies
carry	carries	carries
hanky	hankies	hankies
poppy	poppies	poppies

2. Add *ing* to the following words. Then rewrite the entire word.

hurry_ing_	hurrying
study_ing_	studying
play_ing_	playing
stay_ing_	staying
worry_ing_	worrying
obey_ing_	obeying

© Teacher Created Materials, Inc. 75 #3240 BBLS—Book 3: Vowel Sounds

Answer Key (cont.)

Page 21

Making "y" Words Plural

Unit 2: Vowels and Word Endings

> **i** Words ending in *y* are also different when they are made plural (more than one).
> Look at the letter before the *y*.
> **r** • If there is a vowel before the *y*, just add the ending *s*.
> Example: monkey → monkeys
> • If there is a consonant before the *y*, change the *y* to *i* and add *es*.
> Example: lady → ladies

1. Make these words plural (more than one).

puppy	puppies	baby	babies
pony	ponies	lady	ladies
penny	pennies	doggy	doggies
donkey	donkies	monkey	monkies

2. Make a new word by adding one of the suffixes *ing*, *er*, *ness*, or *est* to each of the following words. (Remember: if the suffix begins with a consonant or *i*, do not change the *y*.) Don't write the same word twice.

worry	worrying	funny	funniest
hurry	hurrying	vary	varying
merry	merriest	funny	funnier
dusty	dustiest	copy	copying
dry	drying	dry	drier
happy	happier	happy	happiest
messy	messier	messy	messiest
angry	angrier	lazy	laziness
empty	emptier	hungry	hungriest

Page 22

Words with "ight"

Unit 2: Vowels and Word Endings

> **i** The rime pattern *igh* says /i/ as in *five*. The rime pattern *ight* is used in many words. Think of *nightlight*. It has the *ight* pattern twice!

1. Find eight words that have *ight* as their rime. Use the consonant and consonant blend lists to help you.

fight	bright	sight	tight
light	right	might	flight

2. Choose the best word to complete the sentence then cross out the other words.

   a. The boys began ~~fight~~ ~~fights~~ **fighting** after the football match.
   b. The stage lights needed **bright** ~~brighten~~ ~~brightening~~ so the actors could be seen.
   c. King Arthur had many ~~night~~ ~~nights~~ **knights** who were mighty fighting men.
   d. The rubbish at the seaside is ~~sights~~ ~~sightly~~ **unsightly**. It blemishes the sandy beaches.
   e. The little baby was ~~fright~~ **frightened** ~~frights~~ of the dark.

3. Add one of the suffixes *ful*, *less*, *ly*, *en*, or *ness* to the words so each sentence makes sense.

   a. The dodo was a bird that could not fly. It was flight **less**.
   b. The bright **ness** of the light made my eyes sting.
   c. I felt slight **ly** ill after being on the high roller coaster.
   d. Tight **en** the lid before the juice drips out.
   e. What a fright **ful** mess in here. Get it cleaned up.

Page 23

"y" Word Poetry

Unit 2: Vowels and Word Endings

Read the words then use them to complete each line of the poems.

1. trying — denying — frying — crying

   There is no _____ **denying**
   It is rather _____ **trying**.
   When onions are _____ **frying**
   You always end up _____ **crying**.

2. mummy — happiest — hungriest — tummy

   The baby's not at his _____ **happiest**
   When he's at his _____ **hungriest**
   The emptier his _____ **tummy**
   The more he cries like a _____ **mummy**.

3. funny — shy — why — sunny

   On days that were hot and _____ **sunny**
   The clown didn't feel nearly as _____ **funny**
   He said the sun just made him _____ **shy**
   But what he couldn't say was _____ **why**.

Page 25

Reading "ew" and "oo"

Unit 3: "ew" and "oo"

> **i** There are two ways of saying *oo*:
> • /u/ as in *foot*
> • /oo/ as in *boot* and *new*.
> Example: I need a new *boot* for my *foot*.

1. Underline the *oo* and *ew* in these one-syllable words. Then look, say, listen, cover, write, and check, putting the word into the correct box below.

food	grew	look	few	wood
threw	loose	good	goose	stood
choose	tooth	wool	took	chew
soon	room	crew	cook	stew

/oo/ as in "boot"	/u/ as in "foot"
choose goose	look took
soon food	good cook
loose tooth	wool wood
room	stood

/oo/ as in "crew"
threw crew
grew chew
few stew

2. Add a different suffix to each word so it makes sense. Choose *er*, *less*, *y*, *ing*, *en*, or *ish*. Some will have more than one right answer.

room **y**	sleep **ing**	tooth **less**
cook **ing**	wood **en**	look **ing**
fool **ish**	self **ish**	self **less**
point **less**	mood **y**	sweep **ing**

Answer Key (cont.)

Page 26

Unit 3: "ew" and "oo"

Writing with "ew" and "oo"

1. Complete the sentences using your own words.
   a. Have you _____ my new _____?
   b. The crew _____ were pulling _____.
   c. I knew _____ so I _____.
   d. I threw _____ so hard that it _____.
   e. You must not chew _____, otherwise you'll _____.
   f. There are a few _____. Would you like _____?
   g. If I could choose my _____ I would _____.

2. Underline the *oo* in these two-syllable words. Then look, say, listen, cover, write, and check!

gl**oo**m	y	gloomy
bab	**oo**n	baboon
tat	t**oo**	tattoo
mon	s**oo**n	monsoon
mush	r**oo**m	mushroom
p**oo**	dle	poodle
n**oo**	dles	noodles
bal	l**oo**ns	balloons
bas	s**oo**n	bassoon
coc	**oo**n	cocoon
pre	sch**oo**l	preschool
f**oo**l	ish	foolish
car	t**oo**n	cartoon

Page 27

Unit 3: "ew" and "oo"

Two-Syllable "oo" Words

1. Match the syllables to make a real word.

   a.
   - bal — oon → balloon
   - lag — room → lagoon
   - mon — phoon → monsoon
   - soo — ner → sooner
   - mush — dle → mushroom
   - poo — soon → poodle
   - ty — loon → typhoon

   b.
   - roo — loo → rooster
   - ig — oon → igloo
   - sal — lish → saloon
   - mar — toon → maroon
   - foo — soon → foolish
   - car — oon → cartoon
   - bas — ster → bassoon

2. Mark the vowels and consonants and find where each word is divided into syllables. (Remember: start from the first vowel.) Write the syllables on the lines.

	1st	2nd		1st	2nd
balloon	bal	loon	voodoo	voo	doo
shampoo	sham	poo	lagoon	la	goon
igloo	ig	loo	mushroom	mush	room
cocoon	co	coon	toothache	tooth	ache
noodle	noo	dle	baboon	ba	boon
platoon	pla	toon	festoon	fes	toon
typhoon	ty	phoon	saloon	sal	oon
poodle	poo	dle	cartoon	car	toon

Page 28

Unit 3: "ew" and "oo"

More "oo," "ew," and "ui"

1. As you read the story, underline the words that contain *oo* or *ew*. Write your own ending for the story.

   It was late <u>afternoon</u> when my brother, the <u>fool</u>, <u>threw</u> the <u>boomerang</u>. It should have curved back, but it didn't. Just like a <u>new</u> <u>harpoon</u>, it hit the <u>kangaroo</u> between the eyes. The <u>kangaroo</u> <u>looked</u> up and <u>zoomed</u> towards us like a steam train. He <u>looked</u> like Road Runner, the <u>cartoon</u> character. <u>Doom</u> was near! I didn't bother to rinse the <u>shampoo</u> from my hair. I grabbed the packet of <u>macaroons</u> from the table and <u>threw</u> them in his path, hoping he would stop to <u>chew</u> them. He _____

   i The vowels *ui* together say /oo/ as in *boot*.

2. In the following words *ui* says /oo/ as in *boot*. Practice reading these words and trace over each word three times. Then look, say, listen, cover, write, and check!

fruit	fruit	suit	suit	juice	juice
bruise	bruise	cruise	cruise	recruit	recruit

3. Use the words above to complete the sentences.
   a. The waiter spilled the ___fruit___ ___juice___ down the front of my ___suit___.
   b. I got a ___bruise___ on my arm when the ___cruise___ ship banged into the rocks.

Page 29

Unit 3: "ew" and "oo"

"ew" and "oo" Poetry

1. hero — moon — soon — zero

   The rocket will set off ___soon___
   On its final flight to the ___moon___.
   The astronaut will be a ___hero___
   Five, four, three, two, one, ___zero___.

2. chew — crew — barbecue — avenue

   If you continue up the ___avenue___
   You'll catch the scent of a ___barbecue___.
   Just go inside and say hello to the ___crew___
   There's plenty of food to bite and ___chew___.

3. spoon — moon — buffoon — afternoon

   There was a silly ___buffoon___
   Who wanted to fly to the ___moon___.
   Except he was traveling by ___spoon___,
   And he fell back to Earth by ___afternoon___.

Answer Key (cont.)

Page 31

Unit 4: "ou"/"ow" and "oi"/"oy"

Words with "ou" and "ow"

> The vowels *ou* and *ow* stay together in one syllable and say /ow/ as in *cow*.
> Example: Do not *shout* at that *cow*.

1. Add *ou* or *ow* to the following letters to make real words. Make sure they look right. Then look, say, listen, cover, write, and check!

c_ow_	cow	_ou_t	out
l_ow_	low	br_ow_	brow
f_ou_nd	found	h_ow_	how
r_ow_	row	s_ow_	sow
n_ow_	now	ab_ou_t	about
r_ou_nd	round	m_ou_th	mouth
v_ow_	vow	tr_ou_sers	trousers
ar_ou_nd	around	acc_ou_nt	account
m_ou_se	mouse	h_ou_se	house

2. Write down words that rhyme with the words below.

sound	shout	now
bound	about	cow
found	snout	how
ground	spout	plow
pound	trout	vow

Page 32

Unit 4: "ou"/"ow" and "oi"/"oy"

More Words with "ou" and "ow"

> The letters *ow* are found in the middle of a word before *l*, *n*, and *er*.

1. Draw a line from the consonants to the rimes to make words. Then write the words on the blank lines. The first one is done for you.

- cl — clown
- br — brown
- d — own
- dr — drown
- t — town

- fl — flower
- p — power
- sh — shower
- ower

- h — howl
- f — owl, fowl
- gr — growl

2. Add the endings *ing* and *ed* to the following words. Then use one of the words to complete the sentence.

	Add *ing*.	Add *ed*.
a. shout	shouting	shouted
The man was shouting at me to stop.
b. sound	sounding	sounded
The pop music sounded very loud and deafened me.
c. cloud	clouding	clouded
The sky was clouding over and it began to rain.
d. scowl	scowling	scowled
The bank robber scowled at the cashier.
e. shower	showering	showered
We take turns getting showered every morning.
f. allow	allowing	allowed
I was never allowed to chew gum in school.

Page 33

Unit 4: "ou"/"ow" and "oi"/"oy"

Words with "oi" and "oy"

> The letters *oi* and *oy* stay together in one syllable and say /oy/ as in *boy*.
> Example: The *boy points*.
> (Note: The letters *oi* are never found at the end of a word.)

1. Add the vowel pattern *oi* or *oy* to complete these one-syllable words. Make sure they look right. Then look, say, listen, cover, write, and check!

s_oy_	soy	b_oi_l	boil
c_oi_l	coil	j_oy_	joy
j_oi_nt	joint	m_oi_st	moist
b_oy_	boy	j_oi_n	join
sp_oi_l	spoil	t_oy_	toy
n_oi_se	noise	p_oi_nt	point
ch_oi_ce	choice	v_oi_ce	voice

2. Use the words above to complete these sentences.
   a. The **boy** was making too much **noise** with the trumpet.
   b. The tissue was **moist** after wiping up the spilled **soy** milk.
   c. It is a **joy** to listen to a beautiful singing **voice**.
   d. If you **boil** cabbage too long it will **spoil**.
   e. "Please **point** to the candy of your **choice**," said the shopkeeper.
   f. We will have to use a **coil** of wire to fix the **toy**.

Page 34

Unit 4: "ou"/"ow" and "oi"/"oy"

More Words with "oi" and "oy"

1. Match the syllables to make a real word.

a.
- ap — joy, appoint
- em — noy, employ
- an — point, annoy
- en — ploy, enjoy

b.
- de — joice, decoy
- a — coy, avoid
- re — void, rejoice
- un — load, unload

2. Use the words above to complete the sentences.
   a. You **annoy** me by talking too much.
   b. I always try to **avoid** danger and housework!
   c. People **rejoice** at the birth of a baby.
   d. The court will **appoint** a lawyer to the case.
   e. The noise was a **decoy** so the robbers could get into the bank.
   f. I **enjoy** playing sports, especially soccer.
   g. The company was able to **employ** fifteen hundred workers.

3. Read each syllable. Then rearrange them so they make a word you recognize.

point – ap – dis	disappoint
i – nois – ly	noisily
ment – ap – point	appointment
ploy – er – em	employer
troy – des – er	destroyer
ee – em – ploy	employee

Answer Key (cont.)

Page 35

Vowel Sound Poetry
Unit 4: "ou"/"ow" and "oi"/"oy"

Read the words in this box. Then use them to complete each line of the poems.

1. out — sound — round — sprout

   At dinner one night, I ate a bad ___sprout___.
   As soon as it went in, it wanted to come ___out___.
   It churned inside, going round and ___round___.
   It even caused a strange gurgling ___sound___.

2. enjoying — appointment — ointment — annoying

   The dance I was ___enjoying___
   When I tripped, which was ___annoying___
   Then I had to make an ___appointment___
   At the doctors for some ___ointment___.

3. loyal — flower — royal — flour

   The king, who was quite ___royal___
   Asked the baker, who was very ___loyal___
   To bake him a cake of sugar and ___flour___
   And decorated with the petals of a ___flower___.

Page 37

Three-Syllable Words
Unit 5: Three-Syllable Vowel Sounds

ℹ Three-syllable words have three beats when you say them, so they can be split into three parts. There is a vowel sound in every beat.

1. Say each syllable and combine them to make a word. Then look, say, listen, cover, write, and check!

No•vem•ber	November
Oc•to•ber	October
re•mem•ber	remember
bas•ket•ball	basketball
la•bor•er	laborer
ro•man•tic	romantic
e•quip•ment	equipment
ver•ti•cal	vertical

2. Read the words again. Make sure you know what they all mean.

3. Write each syllable of the words above under the correct type of syllable.

Open syllable (ends in vowel)	Vowel + r syllable (ends with vowel + r)	Closed syllable (ends in consonant)	
No	ber	vem	man
to	ber	Oc	tic
re	ber	mem	quip
la	bor	bas	ment
ro	er	ket	tic
e	ver	ball	al

Page 38

Dividing Three Syllables
Unit 5: Three-Syllable Vowel Sounds

Mark the vowels first, then mark the consonants and decide where to split the words into syllables (beats).

VC Pattern	1st Beat	2nd Beat	3rd Beat	Cover, Write, and Check
fantastic	fan	tas	tic	fantastic
estimate	es	tim	ate	estimate
vitamins	vi	ta	mins	vitamins
illustrate	il	lus	trate	illustrate
pendulum	pen	du	lum	pendulum
hexagon	hex	a	gon	hexagon
consider	con	si	der	consider
parallel	par	al	lel	parallel
capital	cap	i	tal	capital
positive	pos	i	tive	positive
infantile	in	fan	tile	infantile
badminton	bad	min	ton	badminton
components	com	po	nents	components
kilogram	kil	o	gram	kilogram
examine	ex	am	ine	examine
unison	un	i	son	unison
negative	neg	a	tive	negative

Read the words again. Make sure you know the meaning of all these words. Look in a dictionary if you don't.

Page 39

Using Three-Syllable Words
Unit 5: Three-Syllable Vowel Sounds

1. Read the words. They are split up into their syllables.

un•der•stand	im•por•tant	o•ver•come
dis•em•bark	ar•gu•ment	im•mor•tal
im•pro•vise	in•ter•act	dif•fer•ent
im•pro•vise	in•ter•est	sep•ar•ate

2. Use the words above to complete the sentences below. Use a dictionary to help you. The sentences must make sense.

   a. My hobby and ___interest___ is collecting shells.
   b. I shall have to ___separate___ you two if you do not stop talking when I am trying to give a lesson.
   c. The movie had no script. The actors were asked to ___improvise___ their roles.
   d. We had to ___disembark___ from the ship at 10 o'clock.
   e. The old lady died because she had been ___overcome___ by the fumes from the fire.
   f. My black socks are ___different___ than your white socks.
   g. The boy was ___desperate___ to get his bike back before his mom found that it was missing.
   h. We had an ___argument___ about who was going to wash up first.
   i. Children need to learn how to ___interact___ with others.
   j. 007 James Bond seems ___immortal___. He never dies in his films.
   k. It is ___important___ that you ___understand___ what I am saying.

Answer Key (cont.)

Page 40

Unit 5: Three-Syllable Vowel Sounds

Understanding Three-Syllable Words

1. Match the words to their meanings. You may need to use a dictionary.

   a.
Word	Meaning
negative	make up for
estimate	1,000 grams
components	guess
kilogram	minus
compensate	parts

   Matches: negative—minus; estimate—guess; components—parts; kilogram—1,000 grams; compensate—make up for

   b.
Word	Meaning
vitamins	outside something
external	straight up
internal	inspect
vertical	goodness in food
examine	inside something

   Matches: vitamins—goodness in food; external—outside something; internal—inside something; vertical—straight up; examine—inspect

2. Choose one of the words above to complete the following sentences.
   a. A **kilogram** bag of sugar holds the same as 1,000 grams.
   b. -3 is a **negative** number.
   c. A **vertical** line goes up and down.
   d. Please **estimate** the height of the room in feet.
   e. The electrical **components** in a computer are very small.
   f. Sun screen is for **external** use only.
   g. I want you to **compensate** me for my pen that you lost.
   h. We should all eat fresh foods so we know we are getting the minerals and **vitamins** we need.
   i. The heart is an **internal** organ.
   j. **Examine** your change before leaving the shop, as mistakes cannot be rectified.

Page 41

Unit 5: Three-Syllable Vowel Sounds

Three-Syllable Poetry

Read the words then use them to complete each line of the poems.

1. romantic — surprise — Atlantic — paradise

   It was very __**romantic**__
   To cruise across the __**Atlantic**__.
   It was a great __**surprise**__
   To be a guest in __**paradise**__.

2. do — regular — muscular — two

   If I want to make my body __**muscular**__
   I have to keep my exercise __**regular**__.
   I must lose a pound or __**two**__
   Follow a diet is what I'll __**do**__.

3. comical — monocle — bicycle — maniacal

   Some say he looks __**maniacal**__
   Pedaling so fast on his __**bicycle**__.
   Others say he's just __**comical**__
   Squinting through one large __**monocle**__.

Notes